Men of the African Ark

Photographs by
ANGELA FISHER and
CAROL BECKWITH

Pomegranate

SAN FRANCISCO

Pomegranate
Box 6099, Rohnert Park, CA 94927

Pomegranate Europe Ltd., Fullbridge House, Fullbridge
Maldon, Essex CM9 4LE, England

ISBN 0-7649-0371-3
Pomegranate Catalog No. A914

Photographs are from the private collection of Angela Fisher and Carol Beckwith and from
Maasai (1980), *Nomads of Niger* (1983), *Africa Adorned* (1984), and *African Ark* (1990),
published by The Harvill Press in the United Kingdom and Harry N. Abrams in the
United States. The private collection of Fisher/Beckwith photographs is handled by the
Robert Estall Library, Suffolk, England (tel. 44-1787-210111; fax 44-1787-211440).

Pomegranate publishes books of postcards on a wide range of subjects.
Please write to the publisher for more information.

Designed by Elizabeth Key
Printed in Korea
06 05 04 03 02 01 00 99 98   10 9 8 7 6 5 4 3 2

BETWEEN THE EAST AND WEST COASTS OF AFRICA lies a cradle of humanity containing a richly diverse mix of peoples and cultures. From the nomads of the desert to the settled communities of the equatorial forest, ceremony and ritual are vital to life, and passages are marked by elaborate celebrations.

Through rites and initiations, the men of the Ark express their creativity and their roles within their cultures. The breadth and diversity of expression encompass the rolling eyes and flashing teeth of the Wodaabe charm dancers of Niger, the golden regalia of the Ashanti of Ghana, the colorful beaded bodices of the Dinka of Sudan, and the striking painted faces of the Karo of Ethiopia.

Carol Beckwith and Angela Fisher journeyed from the Omo River region of Ethiopia to the Sahel of West Africa and from the Maasai plains of Kenya to the Royal Akan Kingdom of Ghana to photograph the lives, customs, and ceremonies of the men of Africa. This beautiful book of postcards provides a glimpse into an astonishing variety of fascinating cultures.▼

CAROL BECKWITH was born and educated in the United States. Since 1972 she has traveled throughout Africa, living with the Maasai of Kenya and Tanzania and the Wodaabe of Niger. These experiences led to her two photographic books, *Maasai* (with Tepilit Ole Saitoti, 1980), which received the Annisfield-Wolf Award in Race Relations, and *Nomads of Niger* (with Marion van Offelen, 1984), which became the subject of her award-winning film *Way of the Wodaabe* (1988). Between 1988 and 1990 she co-produced two programs about the Wodaabe for the television series *Millennium* and collaborated with Angela Fisher on *The Painter and the Fighter*, a film about the Surma of Ethiopia. Her most recent book, *African Ark* (1990), was the result of a five-year collaboration with Angela Fisher. Carol's photographs have been exhibited and published in the United States, Europe, Japan, and Africa.

ANGELA FISHER was born and educated in Australia. Since 1970 she has spent most of her time in Africa. Her first book, *Africa Adorned* (1984), a photographic record of the jewelry and body decorations of the peoples of the African continent, was featured in the November 1986 issue of *National Geographic* magazine. She has also photographed traditional ceremonies and everyday life in Yemen, Afghanistan, Nepal, Ladakh, and India, and her photographs and collections of ethnic jewelry have been exhibited in Europe, the United States, Canada, Kenya, and Australia. Angela collaborated with Carol Beckwith on *African Ark* (1990), a book about the peoples and cultures of the Horn of Africa. This work led to *The Painter and the Fighter*, a film about the Surma, one of the most remote peoples of Ethiopia.

AT PRESENT Carol and Angela are working on *African Ceremonies*, a book about the traditional life cycles of peoples of the African continent due to be published in 1998 by Harry N. Abrams.

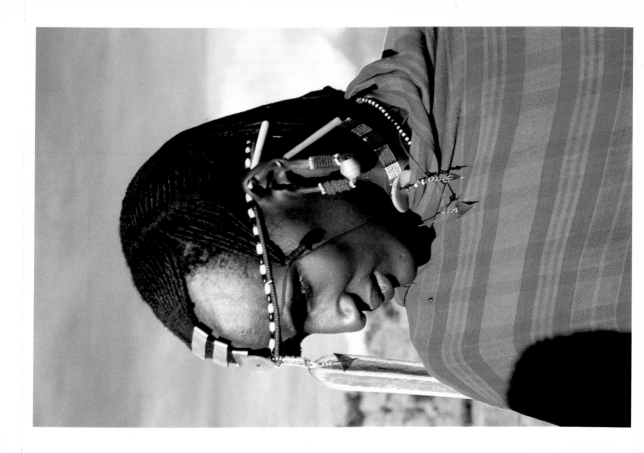

Men of the African Ark

PHOTOGRAPHS BY CAROL BECKWITH
AND ANGELA FISHER

MAASAI WARRIOR, Kenya

To become a warrior is the dream of every Maasai youth.
A warrior must be strong, clever, courageous, wise, and
gentle. He must hunt lions for his headdress, protect his
herds from predators, and safeguard his community. This
young warrior wears the ocher makeup and ornamentation
that mark his status.

POMEGRANATE   BOX 6099   ROHNERT PARK CA 94927

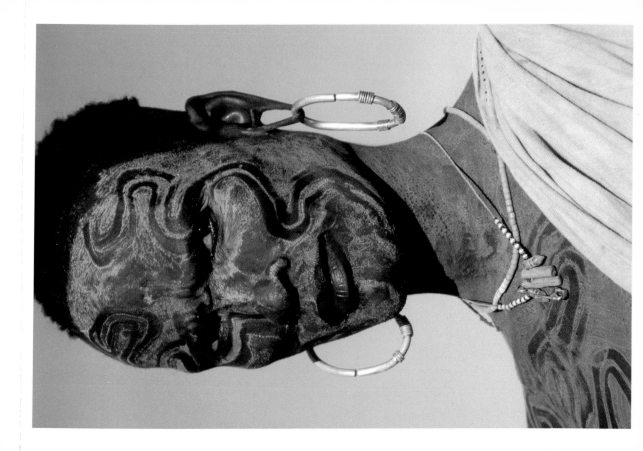

Men of the African Ark

PHOTOGRAPHS BY CAROL BECKWITH
AND ANGELA FISHER

SURMA STICK FIGHTER, Ethiopia

Face paint and a fierce expression are intended to intimidate the opponent of a *Donga* stick fighter. The fights are held to prove masculinity, settle vendettas, and win wives. This champion fighter has the privilege of choosing a wife from a select group of girls in his village.

POMEGRANATE BOX 6099 ROHNERT PARK CA 94927

Men of the African Ark

PHOTOGRAPHS BY CAROL BECKWITH
AND ANGELA FISHER

TUAREG NOMAD ON A CAMEL, Niger

A Tuareg nomad from the Sahara Desert arrives in full
regalia to join his Wodaabe neighbors as they celebrate
the rainy season.

POMEGRANATE BOX 6099 ROHNERT PARK CA 94927

Men of the African Ark

PHOTOGRAPHS BY ANGELA FISHER
AND CAROL BECKWITH

ROYAL KATSINA CAVALIER, Nigeria

Honoring their proud military tradition at the annual
Sallah ceremony, members of the cavalry of the Emir of
Katsina are resplendent in chain mail tunics, indigo turbans,
and silver talismans.

POMEGRANATE   BOX 6099   ROHNERT PARK, CA 94927

Men of the African Ark

PHOTOGRAPHS BY CAROL BECKWITH
AND ANGELA FISHER

KARO MAN WITH A PAINTED HANDPRINT
DESIGN, Ethiopia

The pattern of each Karo body painting is highly decorative
and changes daily. No two designs are the same. This man
is particularly proud of his unique handprint motif, featured
on both his front and his back.

POMEGRANATE   BOX 6099   ROHNERT PARK CA 94927

Men of the African Ark

PHOTOGRAPHS BY ANGELA FISHER
AND CAROL BECKWITH

SURMA STICK FIGHT, Ethiopia

The *Donga* stick fight is one of the most dangerous sports on the African continent. There are no rules except that a man must not kill his opponent.

POMEGRANATE   BOX 6099   ROHNERT PARK   CA 94927

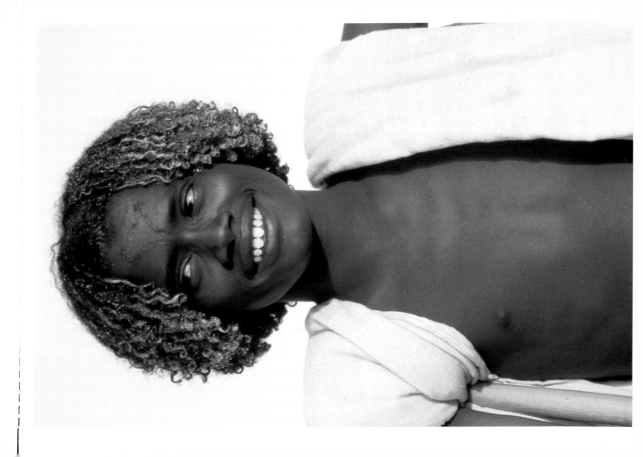

Men of the African Ark

PHOTOGRAPHS BY ANGELA FISHER
AND CAROL BECKWITH

YOUNG AFAR MAN, Ethiopia

The Afar are a handsome race; their skin tones vary from
copper red to deep brown, and their features are finely
chiseled. To protect their skin from the harsh environment
of the Danikil Desert, they coat themselves liberally with
animal fat.

POMEGRANATE BOX 6099 ROHNERT PARK CA 94927

Men of the African Ark

PHOTOGRAPHS BY CAROL BECKWITH
AND ANGELA FISHER

KARO DANCER WITH SPOTTED BODY
PAINT, Ethiopia

The striking face and body decoration of this Karo man
is inspired by the spotted plumage of the guinea fowl,
a species indigenous to the Omo River region.

POMEGRANATE BOX 6099 ROHNERT PARK CA 94927

Men of the African Ark

PHOTOGRAPHS BY CAROL BECKWITH
AND ANGELA FISHER

WODAABE MAN PREPARING FOR A CHARM DANCE, Niger

The Wodaabe nomads of Niger have a unique way of attracting wives: they spend hours beautifying themselves in preparation for an all-male charm dance. The women serve as judges for this dance and select their husbands and lovers from among the contestants.

POMEGRANATE BOX 6099 ROHNERT PARK CA 94927

Men of the African Ark

PHOTOGRAPHS BY CAROL BECKWITH
AND ANGELA FISHER

ASHANTI SWORD BEARER, Ghana

Preceding the Ashanti king at royal ceremonies, the chief
sword bearer is recognizable by his tall eagle-feather headdress with its gold-leaf ram's horn. Carrying the *Sword
of Allegiance*, he symbolizes spiritual protection for the
ceremony as well as for the entire Ashanti nation.

POMEGRANATE BOX 6099 ROHNERT PARK CA 94927

Men of the African Ark

PHOTOGRAPHS BY CAROL BECKWITH
AND ANGELA FISHER

MAASAI ELDER, Tanzania

Elderhood marks a period of responsibility in the life of a
Maasai man. Beginning with marriage, it continues with
the building of a family home and the acquisition of wealth
in the form of children and cattle.

POMEGRANATE   BOX 6099   ROHNERT PARK CA 94927

Men of the African Ark

PHOTOGRAPHS BY CAROL BECKWITH
AND ANGELA FISHER

WINNERS OF A WODAABE CHARM DANCE, Niger

During the *Yaake* charm dance, Wodaabe male dancers
try to surpass one another in personality and magnetism.
Standing side by side and facing their audience, they widen
their eyes and show off their teeth in broad, exaggerated
smiles. A man who can hold one eye still as he rolls the
other one is considered especially alluring.

POMEGRANATE BOX 6099 ROHNERT PARK, CA 94927

Men of the African Ark

PHOTOGRAPHS BY ANGELA FISHER
AND CAROL BECKWITH

DECORATED KARO MAN, Ethiopia

Just as chalk is used to decorate the face, clay is used to
fashion the elaborate hairstyles of Karo men. This man's
hair bun may have taken as long as three days to perfect.

POMEGRANATE BOX 6099 ROHNERT PARK, CA 94927

Men of the African Ark

PHOTOGRAPHS BY CAROL BECKWITH
AND ANGELA FISHER

HAUSA MAN WITH HIS HORSE, Nigeria

Every year at the end of Ramadan, thousands of Hausa and Fulani horsemen decorate their mounts to prepare for presentation to the Emir of Katsina as part of the *Sallah* ceremony.

POMEGRANATE BOX 6099 ROHNERT PARK CA 94927

Men of the African Ark

PHOTOGRAPHS BY ANGELA FISHER
AND CAROL BECKWITH

SURMA MAN, Ethiopia

In preparation for the *Donga* stick fights, Surma men paint themselves from head to toe. They smear their bodies with a mixture of chalk and water and then draw designs with their fingertips, exposing the dark skin beneath in an intricate pattern of lines. By doing this, they hope to make themselves not only more attractive to women but also more fearsome to their opponents.

POMEGRANATE BOX 6099 ROHNERT PARK CA 94927

Men of the African Ark

PHOTOGRAPHS BY CAROL BECKWITH
AND ANGELA FISHER

KARO MEN AT A COURTSHIP DANCE, Ethiopia

Among all the peoples of the Omo River region, the Karo
excel in face and torso painting. Elaborate face masks are
created with locally found white chalk, yellow mineral
rock, pulverized iron ore, and black charcoal. Ostrich
feathers are worn as an indication of bravery, adding a
finishing touch to the overall effect.

POMEGRANATE   BOX 6099   ROHNERT PARK CA 94927

Men of the African Ark

PHOTOGRAPHS BY CAROL BECKWITH
AND ANGELA FISHER

ASHANTI FETISH PRIEST, Ghana

At all important ceremonies, Ashanti fetish priests gather
together to invoke the spirits of their ancestors. Sprinkled
with white clay powder to signify their spiritual purity, they
perform sacred rituals to appease the gods.

POMEGRANATE   BOX 6099   ROHNERT PARK CA 94927

Men of the African Ark

PHOTOGRAPHS BY ANGELA FISHER
AND CAROL BECKWITH

WODAABE MAN WRAPPING HIS TURBAN, Niger

Conforming to an ideal passed down through the genera-
tions, a Wodaabe man takes great care to emphasize his
physical beauty. Pale yellow powder lightens his skin tone,
borders of black kohl highlight his eyes and teeth, and a
painted line elongates his nose. He completes his look by
swathing his head in a turban fashioned from a twelve-foot
length of cloth.

POMEGRANATE BOX 6099 ROHNERT PARK CA 94927

Men of the African Ark

PHOTOGRAPHS BY CAROL BECKWITH
AND ANGELA FISHER

KARO MAN PREPARING FOR A COURTSHIP DANCE, Ethiopia

The Karo, one of the smallest ethnic groups along the Omo River, are renowned for their elaborate face painting.

POMEGRANATE   BOX 6099   ROHNERT PARK   CA   94927

Men of the African Ark

PHOTOGRAPHS BY CAROL BECKWITH
AND ANGELA FISHER

YAAKE CHARM DANCE, Niger

At the *Yaake* dance, handsome young Wodaabe men vie
for the honor of being judged the most charming and
charismatic, thus proving their outstanding ability to
attract women.

POMEGRANATE   BOX 6099   ROHNERT PARK, CA 94927

Men of the African Ark

PHOTOGRAPHS BY ANGELA FISHER
AND CAROL BECKWITH

ASHANTI KING RIDING ON A PALANQUIN, Ghana

King Otumfuo Opuko Ware II of Ghana celebrates the
twenty-fifth anniversary of his reign with a sumptuous display
of gold, reaffirming the power of his ancient kingdom.

POMEGRANATE   BOX 6099   ROHNERT PARK, CA 94927

Men of the African Ark

PHOTOGRAPHS BY ANGELA FISHER
AND CAROL BECKWITH

KARO PAINTED MAN, Ethiopia

As red ocher, yellow, and white paint transform a Karo
man's body, his spirit is released. Here, ostrich feathers,
worn as an indication of bravery, are placed in a gray-and-
ocher clay hair bun, which signifies that its wearer has
killed an enemy or a dangerous animal.

POMEGRANATE   BOX 6099   ROHNERT PARK CA 94927

Men of the African Ark

PHOTOGRAPHS BY CAROL BECKWITH
AND ANGELA FISHER

AKAN CHIEF RIDING ON A PALANQUIN, Ghana

During the traditional *Durbar* processions, paramount Akan
chiefs, wearing all their gold finery, are carried on
palanquins under twirling silk or velvet umbrellas.

POMEGRANATE   BOX 6099   ROHNERT PARK, CA 94927

Men of the African Ark

PHOTOGRAPHS BY ANGELA FISHER
AND CAROL BECKWITH

WODAABE MAN PERFORMING THE *YAAKE* CHARM DANCE, Niger

Believing themselves to be the most beautiful people in the world, the Wodaabe say that their distinctive looks are inherited from their earliest ancestors, Adam and Adama. Of all their noble features, however, it is the eyes that initiate seductions and marriages.

POMEGRANATE   BOX 6099   ROHNERT PARK   CA 94927

Men of the African Ark

PHOTOGRAPHS BY CAROL BECKWITH
AND ANGELA FISHER

SURMA MEN APPLYING BODY PAINT, Ethiopia

Body painting is the main form of artistic expression
available to the Surma. The range of designs is limited
only by the imagination of the artist.

POMEGRANATE   BOX 6099   ROHNERT PARK, CA 94927

Men of the African Ark

PHOTOGRAPHS BY CAROL BECKWITH
AND ANGELA FISHER

WODAABE MAN, Niger

As the dry season comes to an end, this Wodaabe man
looks forward to a series of festivals celebrating the coming
rains, on which all life in his arid homeland depends.

POMEGRANATE   BOX 6099   ROHNERT PARK CA 94927

Men of the African Ark

PHOTOGRAPHS BY CAROL BECKWITH
AND ANGELA FISHER

WODAABE DANCER APPLYING MAKEUP, Niger

Carefully applying makeup to enhance his natural beauty,
a Wodaabe man prepares for the annual *Geerewol*
celebration, during which he will compete for the hand
of a wife or lover.

POMEGRANATE BOX 6099 ROHNERT PARK CA 94927

Men of the African Ark

PHOTOGRAPHS BY CAROL BECKWITH
AND ANGELA FISHER

GROUP OF PAINTED KARO MEN, Ethiopia

These Karo men, prepared for courtship dancing, display a
variety of body painting designed to reveal and enhance
their beauty and attract the eye of the opposite sex. The
handprint motif is one of the most popular designs.

POMEGRANATE BOX 6099 ROHNERT PARK CA 94927

Men of the African Ark

PHOTOGRAPHS BY ANGELA FISHER
AND CAROL BECKWITH

KARO DANCER, Ethiopia

Adorned with traditional body paint, this Karo man
prepares for a courtship ritual in which high-spirited
couples perform a rhythmic and pulsating dance, thrusting
their hips against one another. The laughter of the dancers
is matched by the enthusiasm of the spectators, who sing
as they watch, delighted by the spectacle.

POMEGRANATE   BOX 6099   ROHNERT PARK CA 94927

Men of the African Ark

PHOTOGRAPHS BY CAROL BECKWITH
AND ANGELA FISHER

MAASAI WARRIORS PLAITING HAIR, Kenya

At the peak of their physical prowess, Maasai warriors
spend a great deal of time grooming and decorating one
another. They enjoy great comradeship, often sharing
everything from food to girlfriends.

POMEGRANATE   BOX 6099   ROHNERT PARK CA 94927